CORVETTE

THE ALL-AMERICAN SPORTS CAR

CORVETTE

THE ALL-AMERICAN SPORTS CAR

Tony Thacker
Mike Key

OSPREY
AUTOMOTIVE

First published in 1991 by Osprey Publishing
Limited
59 Grosvenor Street
London W1X 9DA

British Library Cataloguing in Publication
Data

Thacker, Tony
    Corvette. The All-American sports car.
    1. Chevrolet Corvette cars, history
    1. Title   II. Key, Mike
    629.2222

    ISBN 1 85532 104 1

Editor Colin Burnham
Page design Angela Posen

Printed in Hong Kong

Front cover
*Andrew Barry's classic 1958 Corvette,
pictured several thousand miles from
its place of manufacture in the wilds
of Essex, England*

Half-title page
*After a quarter of a century of
development, Chevrolet, with its ZR-1,
has produced a no-compromise, world-
class sports car that can stand its
ground amongst the competition. That
intangible quality called class, long
missing from the marque's make-up,
is overshadowed by technical
excellence in everything from fuel
economy to high-speed handling
characteristics. The ZR-1 is not only a
milestone in Corvette history, it is a
landmark in the story of the sports car*

Title page
*1965 Corvette coupe, owned by Colin
Barnard and driven regularly on the
street. Under the bonnet is a 'big
block' 396 cu. in. V8, originally
designed to produce 425 bhp*

Back cover
*In 1979, the year in which Patrick
Konecny's T-top coupe rolled off the
production line, annual sales topped
the 50,000 mark for the first time*

Acknowledgements
I would like to thank Harley J. Earl
and Zora Arkus-Duntov for
providing the impetus to build
America's only true sports car,
likewise all the engineers who
worked for them and followed
them for their efforts in realizing
their own dreams and the dreams of
those two men. I would also like to
thank Kathy Berghoff for leading
me to the Chevrolet Public
Relations office where Ralph J.
Kramer, director of public
relations, Ed Lechtzin and their
ever-helpful staff, allowed me to
rifle through their extensive photo-
library which provided much of the
material used in this book. Thanks
also to every other Corvette
historian who at this stage in the
game made life so much easier with
respect to facts and figures. Thanks
to Chuck Lombardo for access to
the ZR-1 hot rod roadster and to
Philippe 'Fu Fu' Danh for shooting
it.

Tony Thacker

I wish to say a special 'thank you' to
Ray Groves of Corvette Kingdom,
Stalham, Norfolk for putting me in
touch with several clients whose
cars I photographed—likewise many
Corvette owners for sparing the
time and co-operating in the photo-
shoots (especially those whose cars
didn't make it through the editing
process and onto these pages).
Similar thanks must also go to Keith
Beschi of the Classic Corvette Club
UK, Butch and Barb Koennecke and
Thomas Garvin in the USA, and BC
Classic American Automobiles,
London-based importers of classic
Corvettes.

Mike Key

For a catalogue of all books published by Osprey Automotive
please write to:

**The Marketing Manager, Consumer Catalogue Department
Osprey Publishing Ltd, 59 Grosvenor Street, London, W1X 9DA**

Contents

Despite dismal sales initially, Chevrolet forged ahead with its Corvette programme and for the 1954 Motorama series produced several variations on the Corvette theme. Besides removable hard and soft-top Corvettes, which apart from minor details were identical to the production cars, there was a fastback Corvair and the Nomad station wagon

Project Opel

In the immediate post-war euphoria, General Motors emerged as the biggest of The Big Three, reasserting its position with bold jet-stream styling. At the controls of this rocket-ship-on-wheels extravaganza was Harley J. Earl, founder of the Art and Color Section of GM's and, indeed, Motor City's first serious in-house styling studio.

Earl, a California kid, served his apprenticeship as a coachwork designer to the Hollywood set before being hired as a consultant by Lawrence P. Fisher of Cadillac. In the ensuing years at GM, Earl instigated and supervised the styling of undoubtedly the most outrageous automobiles the world will ever see. The Chevrolet Corvette, however, was not one of these.

Unlike his other flamboyant dream cars with their P-38-inspired tail-fins, fastback roofs and liberal use of chrome, Project Opel, as the Corvette was originally known, was simple and uncluttered. True it was bulbous and retained an element of the rocket-ship styling in its tail, as well as enjoying a rather flashy smile. But it was, nevertheless, clean by comparison.

Equally instrumental in the conception of the Corvette was Edward N. Cole. Cole had been heavily involved with the post-war development of Cadillac's overhead valve V8, and once ensconced as Chevrolet's chief engineer, he trebled the

Robert F. McLean's original layout called for a new chassis with the engine placed well forward and the seats well back affording a desirable 50/50 weight distribution

The original Chevrolet Corvette sports car was unveiled at the prestigious Waldorf Astoria Hotel in New York in January, 1953

engineering staff and instigated work on what would become the heart transplant that saved the Corvette: the 265 cu. in. 'small block' V8.

Meanwhile, Earl engaged engineer Robert F. McLean to develop a chassis which would provide the optimum distribution of weight, yet utilize as many production parts as possible. Earl's goal was to build an affordable sports car to trounce the European imports. And build it quickly.

McLean's design called for a Jaguar XK120 wheelbase of 120 in., a wide track, seats positioned well back, and an engine set well forward. A new chassis had to be fabricated to accommodate the engine, and for the first time Chevrolet employed an open driveline. Off the shelf, however, came their 235 cu. in: ohv 'Blue Flame' six cylinder engine and a decidedly un-sporty two-speed Powerglide transmission.

The engine was pepped up at Cole's instigation to produce 150 bhp with a high-lift, long-duration cam, solid lifters, and an 8:1 compression head. A special aluminium manifold with triple carbs was added and the front of the valve cover was shaved for hood clearance. The Powerglide was utilised since Chevrolet had nothing better available at the time.

Amidst a flurry of publicity, the Corvette was introduced to an apparently enthusiastic public in January, 1953, at the first General Motors Motorama held in the Grand Ballroom of New York's Waldorf-Astoria.

1953–55

Of the reputed four million who saw the new Corvette, raved about it, asked its price and enquired as to when it would be available, few would get to own one. Only 300 were produced and they were more or less hand-built for selected customers. Moreover, there were no plans for a 1954 model.

Earl had wanted a car which cost less than $2,000 (no more than a regular sedan), but by the time the Corvette hit the showrooms the price had risen to almost $3,500.

Meanwhile, the most significant event in the evolution of the Corvette was the arrival, in May 1953, of Zora Arkus-Duntov in the Chevrolet Research and Develoment department...

Above

Despite plans and experiments to build the production Corvette body in steel, it was decided to use glassfibre; an experimental material for automobile bodies at the time. Glassfibre was a fast and easy medium from which to build the Motorama car because it was a fairly simple matter of using the pre-production plaster styling model to create a mould. But when it came to production, Chevrolet had much to learn and the 46 body components for the initial run were produced by Molded Fiber Glass Body Co. of Ashtabula, Ohio. Nevertheless, on June 30, 1953, production began on a six car-long line in a small building adjacent to the Chevrolet plant in Flint, Michigan

Above
Unlike successive Corvettes, the '53, like this example owned by Thomas Garvin, had few options. All were Polo White with Sportsman Red interiors, all had black hoods, and all were equipped with the two options: a heater and a self-seeking AM radio. Of the 300 built about 225 are known to survive

Right
By December, 1953, Chevrolet plant manager Bill Mosher had devised a way to mass-produce the car and production had moved to Chevrolet's St. Louis, Missouri plant where it would continue through November 7, 1969. Minor changes were made, the most noticeable here being the tan top with bows painted to match. Not visible was a running change to a revised camshaft design which increased horsepower to 155. Also for '54 were new body colours of Pennant Blue, Sportsman Red and black. All models had beige tops, red wheels and red interiors with the exception of the blue cars, which had beige interiors

Left

Chevrolet, like most manufacturers, was careful about who took delivery of those early models. Many went to GM managers, VIPs and movie stars who could be guaranteed to generate publicity. This Polo White '54 model was purchased new by actor Errol Flynn and used in several movies. It is now owned by Bob Richie of Minnesota

Above

The big news for 1955 was the September introduction of the overhead valve 265 cu. in. small block V8, instigated by chief engineer, Ed Cole. And it was sorely needed. Production, at around 3,600 units for '54, was well below the projected 20,000 and many of those went unsold. The car was in imminent danger of being axed, but thankfully the decison was never made.

Production in '55 was cut back to a mere 700 units, and a proposed face-lift was dropped. Changes, apart from the now-legendary V8 and relevant insignia, were minor

1956–57

Above

As can be seen from this 1956 model owned by Ian Coombs, little but the basic layout of the dash was held over from previous models. The flush headlights with their sporty stone-guards were replaced by more prominent units. The slab-sided, tub-like body was given shape and speed with a sculpted, chrome-trimmed body cove. The rocket-like tail-fins were shaved to flow with the rear wings, and the tail-lights were tunneled. The exhaust outlets, criticized for 'dirtying' the rear end, were moved outboard and gases now exited through the bumper guards. The boxed license plate from the original '53 Motorama car went, but to prove 'you can't win 'em all' those dummy scoops atop the front wings returned. The twin bulges in the bonnet were said to be inspired by the 1954 Mercedes 300SL. 1956 also marked the arrival of exterior door handles and new hubcaps

Right

Ford, with its late 1954 introduction of the Thunderbird, dealt a body blow to Chevrolet by racking-up sales in 1955 of 16,155 units. Many times more than the Corvette had sold since its introduction. There was now no option but to proceed with a face-lift for '56. Besides, the appointment of Ed Cole as vice-president of GM and general manager of Chevrolet insured the Corvette's future.

Harley Earl already had a re-styled Corvette ready which embodied some styling features previously vetoed because of poor sales. For example, the new model would be available with an optional, removable hard-top seen here in the prototype stage. Note also that this pre-production model does not have the dummy scoops on the wing tops, nor does it feature the chrome trim around the body cove added just prior to production. It does, however, feature roll-up windows

Performance became the watchword in 1956, when Chevy embarked on a publicity-seeking competititive spree under the guidance of Zora Arkus-Duntov. Performance options for '56 included high-lift cams, dual four-barrel carburettors, a close-ratio gearbox, heavy-duty brakes and revised suspension geometry.

Duntov, meanwhile, instigated the construction of the first of three fuel-injected SR-2s (Sebring Racer) for the Sebring 12 Hours of Endurance. The second SR-2 was a road-going coupe for GM President, Harlow Curtice, while the third was a show car for Bill Mitchell. The first car finished 16th at Sebring in 1957.

Seen here at the 1987 Monterey Historic Races, the SR-2 was a basically stock though highly modified competition model raced by Curtis Turner, Dr. Richard Thompson and Harley Earl's son, Jerry

Left

Chevrolet promotional shot from 1957. The 'Ram Jet' fuel injection appraised on the SR-2s found its way into production for '57, though it was not without its problems. Residing atop an enlarged 283 cu. in. V8, the latter became, in Chevy's opinion, the first engine to produce one horsepower per cubic inch. A four-speed manual transmission also became optional as did Posi-traction axles with various ratios, and heavy-duty racing suspension. There was even an EN-engined version available designated 'Not for the Street'

Above

1957 saw Duntov pushing performance even harder. The previous year, he had embarked on the construction of an all-out race car, project XP-64, which became known as the SS (Super Sport). Sporting a tubular frame, de Dion rear suspension and a 307 bhp, fuel-injected V8, two cars were built, one of which was entered in the prototype class for the 1957 Sebring. Unfortunately, despite Juan Manuel Fangio unofficially breaking the Sebring lap record, the SS lasted only 23 laps in the actual race.

Clouds darkened the brightening future of the Corvette, however, with the June, 1957 ban by the Automobile Manufacturers Association on factory involvement in auto racing.

This restored SS was photographed by Kathy Berghoff at the 1987 Monterey Historic Races with John Fitch driving and Duntov himself in the passenger seat

1958–60

Right
Adorned with dummy scoops either side of the grille and in the side coves and simulated hood louvres, the 1958 Corvette garnered an abundance of chrome on its journey through the styling studio, as can be seen on the 'cover car', owned by Andrew Barry. It lost four teeth but it gained two headlights, decorative chrome spears on the boot and almost 200 lb, putting its weight at more than 3000 lb. It also gained some bhp, the most powerful version being rated at 290 bhp

Above
The interior was completely re-designed for 1958, as Mark Phillips' example illustrates. The instruments, with the exception of the clock, were now grouped in front of the driver, either side of a 6000 rpm tachometer and below a semi-circular, 160 mph speedo. A vertical console, housing the heater controls and the Wonder Bar radio, now bridged the gap between the dash and the transmission tunnel. Race-inspired, 'turned' aluminium added to the glitz

Above

In a token effort to re-define the Corvette for 1959, the stylists dispensed with the chrome boot mouldings and the fake bonnet louvres. Other than that, it was a year of minor changes in interior styling to improve driveability and comfort. Door panels and armrests were changed to increase elbow room; for easier reading, gauge lenses were concaved and the tach face re-designed; a storage bin was added beneath the more padded grab bar; a reverse lock-out was added to prevent accidental shifting into reverse

Right

Bill Mitchell's XP-700 caused quite a stir when it first appeared in 1958 because uninformed people thought it was a good indication of the upcoming 1960 production Corvette. It wasn't, but it did pre-empt the shape of the rear end in 1962

Above
If you could see through the skin of Bill Mitchell's Stingray, seen here restored for the 1987 Monterey Historic Races, you'd see the skeleton of Duntov's SS Corvette 'mule'. Mitchell, vice president of styling, spirited the neglected car away to the quasi-secret 'Hammer Room' where it received a new aluminium-reinforced fibreglass body, the lines of which were a precursor of Corvettes to come.

The AMA factory racing ban was still in force, but the Stingray was campaigned privately by Dr. Richard Thompson during 1960 when it achieved the SCCA C-Modified championship

Below

1960 saw the Corvette begin its aluminium diet which continues to this day. First on the menu were heads for the fuel-injected engines. Unfortunately, production problems led to their withdrawal early in the model year. More enduring were new aluminium radiators for Duntov-cammed cars, and ally clutch housings for manual gearboxes. A rear stabilizer, the first on an American car, was also new for 1960

1961–62

Below

The clean-up campaign continued into the 1961 model year with the replacement of all its teeth by a mesh grille first proposed in 1956. The headlight bezels were painted body colour and the rear end was completely re-styled. Inspiration for the re-design came from two sources: the XP-700 show car, and the Stingray racer. The rear now featured a horizontal body line which swept into the rear wheelarch. For the first time, four tail-lights appeared, and they have remained a Corvette trademark ever since. This was the last year for optional wide whitewall tyres but the first year that the exhaust outlets moved underbody

Above

Bill Mitchell's wildest fantasies were exposed in XP-755, initially known as Shark, then Mako Shark I when Mako Shark II debuted in 1965. Elements of the earlier XP-700 remain, but mostly Mako I previewed the forthcoming 1963 Sting Ray

Below
This 1962 example belonging to David Abrahamovitch, is an excellent indicator of how the 'clean' styling continued. Gone is the chrome trim of the side cove, gone with it is the option of contrasting side cove colour. Gone also are the three spears of the simulated vent to be replaced by a multi-finned casting.

The biggest change came under the bonnet where, for the first time, a 327 cu. in. engine became available which, combined with fuel injection, produced 360 bhp. Meanwhile, Semon E. 'Bunkie' Knudsen replaced Ed Cole as Chevrolet general manager and pushed for higher production. The figure rose from 10,939 in 1961 to 14,531 in 1962

Above

Another good preview of upcoming models could be seen in Duntov's Grand Sport effort—his attempt to put a true performance car into production. Manufacturers were, by this time, circumventing the AMA racing ban, and Zora Arkus-Duntov instigated a programme to build 125 (the number needed to qualify as a production sports car), 550 bhp, racing-engined, tube-framed coupes. The plan was nixed by GM management after only five were built, two of which were converted to roadsters for Daytona. The Grand Sports were subsequently sold and successfully raced privately. The two examples seen here were photographed at the 1987 Monterey Historic Races. Number 50 belongs to Jamey Mazzotta, number 2 to Tom Armstrong

1963–64

Below

Though dramatic and bold for its time, the styling of the 'split-window' coupe was the subject of much criticism. Today, however, it forms the trademark of a true 'collector's car' as portrayed by this example belonging to Terry Gibbs. Other distinctive features of the Corvette Sting Ray, as it now became known, were its pivoting quad headlights and doors which cut into the roof. 1963 also saw an end to opening boots and live rear axles

Mechanically the '63 models, with the exception of the transverse-leaf, independent rear suspension, were identical to the '62s. However, power brakes, steering, and air conditioning became optional. The coupes, nevertheless, suffered a ventilation problem partially cured the following year with a three-speed fan

Above
Widely criticized in 1963 was the dual cockpit visible in this roadster owned by Paul Hawkins. Actually, the design merely took the previous effort to its natural conclusion. The instruments, which for this year only, had black faces set in deep aluminium-finish recesses, remain clustered in front of the driver. Also new for '63 were optional leather seats, AM-FM radios and knock-off aluminium wheels

Left
Bill Mitchell's split rear window
bowed to criticism in 1964. Along with
it went the fake bonnet vents, though
the indentations remained. The fake
cockpit vents behind the doors became
real on the driver's side to alleviate
the ventilation problem. Under the
hood, however, 375 bhp was now
available with fuel injection.
Meanwhile, Chevrolet's engineers
concentrated on smoothing-out the
Corvette's rough edges. The '64 coupe
pictured belongs to Chris Sale

Above
Bill Mitchell was hooked on side pipes,
and they popped-up on several show
cars including this one for 1964 which
also sported an egg-crate grille,
another grille on the hood centre with
the words 'fuel injection' on either
side, and altered rear pillar vents

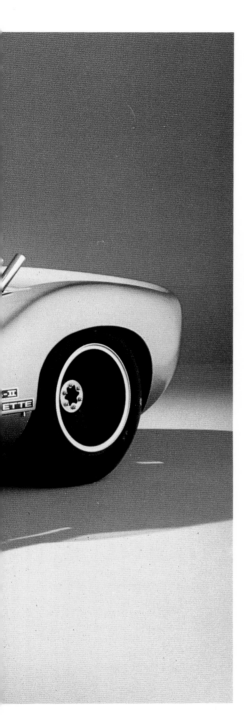

Above

In 1962 Duntov proposed to 'Bunkie' Knudsen a four-wheel drive, mid-engined sports racer to combat Ford's pending GT40 program. Knudsen approved and Duntov proceeded with CERV II. Debuted in 1964, it featured two seats enveloped in full bodywork and was the first mid-engined car in the world to be equipped with full-time, four-wheel drive. Using a 3-valve, 377 cu. in. all-aluminium V8 and separate torque converters (one at each end), CERV II could be geared to do 0 to 60 mph in less than three seconds, or show a top speed of 200 mph. It was also used to evaluate, among other concepts, anti-lift suspension. But when GM hierarchy got wind of the project they nixed it. Both CERV I and II were the subject of a controversy over ownership in the late eighties

Left

Looking a little 'hokey' compared to the purposeful CERV II, this mid-engined mock-up is often mis-credited with being CERV II. According to Duntov, this was a still-born concept produced by Chevrolet R&D

1965–67

Below

The big news for 1965 was the introduction of the 'big-block' 396 cu. in. Mark IV V8. Marketed as the 'Turbo Jet' but known as the 'Porcupine', this engine had been designed from the heads down to produce 425 bhp. It relegated the fuel injection unit a collector's item. To stop the beast, Chevrolet introduced the four-wheel, four-piston disc brakes which ultimately proved leaky and unreliable, and it took the factory almost 20 years to remedy the problem.

Visually, as you can see in these photographs of Colin Barnard's coupe, the car also underwent some physical changes. The hood lost its depressions while the front wing louvres became vertical and functional. Unique to '65 is the grille treatment with black bars and only the outer trim ring bright

Right
Interior changes for 1965 were minimal as can be seen on Gordon Johanson's roadster. Instrument styling now displayed aircraft influence with flat-black faces, the seats were re-designed for improved support, while the door panels became one-piece moulded units

Bill Mitchell's fish fetish surfaced again in 1965 with Mako Shark II, which previewed the 1968 production cars. There were actually two IIs code-named X-15 after the first aircraft to break the sound barrier.

The first, nicknamed the 'pushmobile' for obvious reasons and seen above with 'shark woman', was a show-only car with an aircraft-type steering wheel.

Shark II number two (right) was a running test bed for innovative ideas like the flip-front, digital instruments and retractable 'whaletail' spoiler. The car was powered by a 427 Mk IV which was being phased in as an option for production Vettes

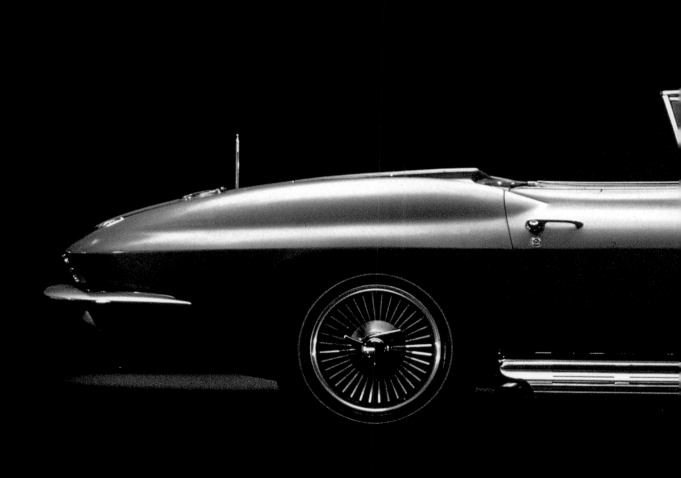

Previous spread
The old dictum 'Don't fix it if it isn't broken' prevailed at Chevrolet as Corvette sales climbed to almost 28,000 units in 1966. Changes were few and geared towards making a good job better. And if big was better, then bigger still must have been even better still, hence the optional 427 cu. in. motor producing 425 bhp. Zero to 60 mph times of 4.8 seconds

and a top speed of 140 mph were recorded. A special hood was fitted to these models but all cars had new egg-crate grilles, new rocker (sill) panels, and reversing lights as standard. The roof vents, both fake and functional, were gone from the coupe

Above
In 1966 these two derivatives of the rear-engined Corvair appeared; the Monza GT (hardtop) and the SS. According to designer Bill Mitchell, because they were lighter, had better aerodynamics and enjoyed superior handling, they could, had not the whole Corvair programme waned, have replaced the Corvette. Or at least have been sold alongside it

Below
The cleaning-up process continued into 1967, when much of the exterior trim went away and the side vents increased in number to five.

Performance was again the big news, and the hot option was the triple-carburettor L-71 which produced 435 bhp. Such Corvettes were sold without heaters supposedly 'to cut down weight and discourage the car's use on the street'

Overleaf
Duntov, despite the various setbacks, continually pushed for a no-compromise Corvette. By that he meant mid-engined, and once engineering ally Ed Cole became president of GM, there began to appear a string of mid-engined concepts which continue to this day with the 1990 showing of CERV III.

The first, dubbed Astro 1, appeared in 1967 and enjoyed many race car and safety-oriented features such as an energy absorbing, adjustable steering column, adjustable pedals, inertia-reel seat belts, roll-over protection, and an anti-surge fuel tank in one sill member.

Chevrolet's 'flowback roof' experiment was powered by a hopped-up, overhead-cam, flat-six Corvair engine. It featured a two-piece fibreglass body, the rear half of which swung back electrically, simultaneously raising the seats to ease entry into a car which stood a mere 35.5 inches high

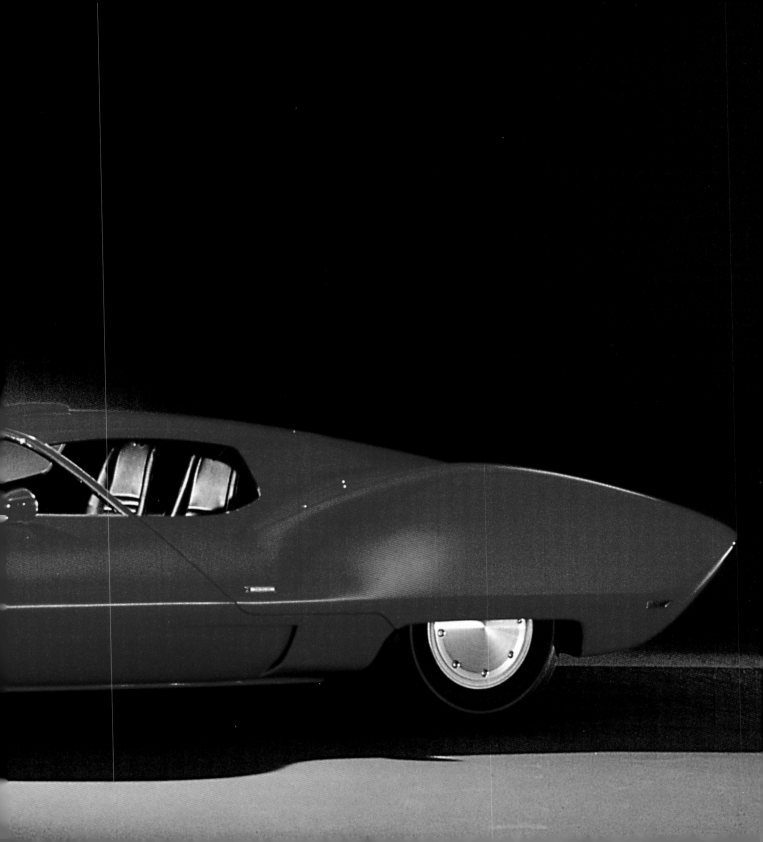

1968–69

Corvette controversy raged once again with the September, 1967 introduction of a complete re-design for 1968. Mitchell's Sting Ray had been replaced by the shark-inspired show cars of 1965.

This totally new, swoopy design, nicknamed 'Coke-bottle', embodied elements from previous concepts yet somehow remained muscular and aesthetically pleasing. Significant points were the removable roof panels and rear window, one-piece side windows, vacuum-operated, pop-up headlights, and wipers hidden behind a vacuum-operated panel that proved troublesome

1968 may have seen some criticism
thrown in the direction of Detroit, but
out of Motor City came yet more
'appetite' concepts. Usually seen in
blue guise, here's a shot of Astro II in
red. Code named XP-880, it utilized a
Lotus-style backbone monocoque
chassis driven through a Pontiac
Tempest transaxle by the ohc Corvair
engine

Nicknamed 'Moby Dick' by GM
stylists, the Astro-Vette was nothing
more than an exercise in
aerodynamics and styling. Make your
own judgments about its enclosed rear
wheels, tapered tail, Moon-style hubcaps, wrap-around windscreen, and
integral roll bar

Above

The word Stingray, missing from the 1968 models, re-appeared in '69 above the side vents as one word, as can be seen on this Sport Coupe owned by Chris Howard. New door handles, new reversing lights integral in the inboard tail-lights, and a new steering/ignition lock, were all minor items when compared to the new 350 cu. in. V8. The 350, which was derived from the 265 introduced in 1955, is still the basic powerplant of production Corvettes, with the exception of the ZR-1.

Despite criticism of the new styling, annual production jumped by another 10,000 units to 38,762

Below
*As always, Duntov was busily heading in a totally different direction. Not happy
with the expensive Corvair assembly used in Astro I and II, Duntov embarked on
two XP-882s—mid-engined projects using mostly off-the-shelf parts.*

*The desired V8 was mounted transversely alongside a chain-driven, stock
Turbo-Hydramatic. The transmission was connected to a stock Corvette
differential via a short, right-angled driveshaft.*

*Though feasible, newly-appointed General Manager John Z. DeLorean
squashed the programme as being impracticable and costly. However, like so
many of Bill Mitchell's 'fishy' concept cars, XP-882 would re-surface*

A preview of the 1970 model appeared as the Aero Coupe in 1969. It had the egg-crate front and side grilles of the forthcoming '70 model, but with additional spoilers, side-pipes and a one-piece roof panel

1970–73

Below
Subtle changes, as seen in Paul Bennett's car, were the order of the day for 1970. Externally, flares were added behind all wheels to prevent debris being kicked-up, new egg-crate grilles for the front and side were added, and for the first time, the Corvette had square rather than round exhaust outlets.

Once again, all the action was under the hood, where there resided a whopping 454 cu. in. V8. Designated LT-1, the production version was rated at 390 bhp. A 460 option was also listed that year, though none are believed to have been factory fitted

Left
The interior was also the subject of change in 1970. In this model owned by Mike Staunton, you can see the 'deluxe' option offered for the first time that year. This included leather seats, wood-grained door panels and console, and special carpets. Tinted glass, four-speed transmissions and Posi-traction all became standard equipment. Due to a late start, production for 1970 fell to 17,316, though November, 1969 saw the 250,000th Corvette roll off the production line

Above
The Aero Coupe was re-worked into the custom-painted Sirocco for 1970. The bumpers were painted, the side-pipe changed, the mirrors were moved up the door pillar, and the roof panel was given a rear-view periscope. This car, like the XP-882, would also see the limelight again, for it was a favourite of Bill Mitchell's

Due to the late introduction of the 1970 model, there are few differences between it and the '71. What changes there were, were under the skin where the fibre optics went in a cost-cutting measure, and horsepower was cut for various economic and environmental reasons. Nevertheless, a ZR1 (sounds familiar?) racing option was available. Included were such goodies as the LT-1 engine, heavy-duty four-speed transmission, heavy-duty power brakes, and sport suspension. All that but no power windows/steering, air conditioning, rear window defogger, wheel covers or radio. For those who preferred the big-block LS-6 option, aluminium heads were now available

Above

DeLorean's hasty squashing of the XP-882 haunted him soon enough when it had to be resurrected in time for the 1970 New York Auto Show to combat Ford's intentions to import the mid-engined De Tomaso Pantera.

As a direct result of this, work began early in 1971 on XP-897GT, another mid-engine concept, this time based around a modified Porsche 914 floorpan and the rotary engine favoured at the time by President Cole. Though not expected to replace the Vette, Bill Mitchell did see it as a possible 'world' sportscar to be built in Germany.

Though styled at GM, the bodywork was executed by Pininfarina in Italy which helps explain how Jaguar Chief Stylist Geoff Lawson, who at the time was working for GM in the UK, found it in a container at a UK GM plant. It almost went to the crusher until Geoff found a willing keeper who, sadly, requested an unrealistic fee to photograph it. Hence this factory shot

Below
*XP-882 revisited. In 1972 the first
XP-882 was resurrected, re-skinned
and re-named XP-895. The basic
transverse powertrain was retained
but the Reynolds Metal Company
added a new aluminium body in an
effort to extol the weight-saving
virtues of that medium. The project
was stillborn. XP-895, however, was
restored by GM employees and
survives to this day*

1972 was a year of lasts for the Corvette. It was the last year for a removable rear window, last year for egg-crate grilles, and the last year for the LT-1 option. It was also the only year, four months actually, when the LT-1 could be ordered with air conditioning. It was, however, the first year for painted front bumpers and a factory-installed anti-theft device

Above
The Mulsanne was the Aero Coupe, which was the Sirocco, fitted with the 'soft' bumpers front and rear destined to appear on the 1973–74 production models. Bill Mitchell called it 'The greatest Stingray ever'

Right
While the federals impacted auto design with their safety and emissions requirements, engineers sought to improve the product. They designed new chassis mounts to isolate road vibrations, and added much sound deadening. To meet safety regulations, a 5 mph impact bumper was added to the front and steel beams were added to the doors to improve side-impact protection. The lifting wiper door was gone but a new bonnet, designed for rear air induction, appeared. Small block power was now provided by the L-82, hydraulic-lifter engine.

Joe Nolosiadly's car was photographed outside the workshops of Corvette Kingdom in Norfolk

Above

1973 also saw the re-emergence of the second XP-882 car, the one DeLorean quashed. Duntov still wanted a mid-engined Corvette, Cole wanted rotary power, so Duntov put the two elements together. With a new swoopy skin from Mitchell's men, he produced Four-Rotor (later called Aerovette) in time for the 1973 Paris Show.

With a 585 cu. in. four-rotor engine in place of the sidewinder V8, it produced 350 bhp at 7,000 rpm. The body, with gullwing doors, worked well in the wind tunnel but the '73 oil crisis put paid to any production prospects (Duntov said fuel consumption averaged 6 mpg). Once again, the mid-engine concept was quashed and Duntov retired soon after. But XP-882 was far from dead

Below
Though Cosworth-Vega based, the
XP-898 is significant because even as
late as 1981 it was rumoured to be the
'shape of Vettes to come'. Basically an
experiment to explore the feasibility
of fibreglass unit construction, it
proved to be strong, light and energy
absorbing

1974–77

Below
1974 was yet another year for firsts and lasts. It was the first year for an impact-absorbing rear bumper, but the last year for genuine dual exhausts. Even worse, the last year for the mighty 454 engine. It would be some time before the Corvette regained its muscles. This roadster belongs to Frazer Wood

Above
Externally, the 1975 Corvette had changed little. There was a new one-piece rear bumper moulding to replace the previous year's two-piece item, while pads were added to the front bumper and L-82 logos appeared on the respective bonnets. Beneath them was either the base L-48, or the L-82. However, there was new 'High Energy Ignition', a catalytic converter, electronic tacho, headlight warning buzzer, and 'Astro-Ventilation'. Something with a fancy name was needed because a true convertible was no longer available

Above

The only visual changes in 1976 were to the front bumper, the rear logo and the rear vents, which went altogether. Not visible was a new steel underbelly which added integrity and isolated the passengers from heat generated by hotter running engines.

The induction system was also re-designed for '76 to allow air to be induced from the front rather than the rear of the hood where it generated excessive noise.

On the subject of noise, the unique Corvette radio disappeared in favour of standard Delco units. The aluminium wheels offered but withdrawn in '73 finally became available. However, to keep the price down, the option included four, not five, wheels. The spare being a standard steel wheel. Finally, there was a new, sealed-for-life battery

Below

Call it Aero Coupe, call it Sirocco, call it Mulsanne; it's all the same car albeit with a new flake 'n' flame paint job. Check the roof line, the periscope, the rear-view mirrors, even the Chaparral wheels. It is the same car

'tarted-up' to commemorate the year of independence. Something new though was the head-up display: a piece of reflective tape on the windscreen to reflect the speedometer reading

Above
Despite more weight and less energy, the Corvette was growing in popularity. Sales had risen steadily through the early seventies and on March 15, 1977, Chevrolet general manager, Robert D. Lund, drove the 500,000th production Corvette off the St. Louis assembly line

Right
Most of the changes for '77 were to the interior where leather seats became standard, and cloth with leather trim optional. A new console housed new heater and air controls; a new push-pull steering wheel had 2 inches of movement; cruise control was introduced; glass roof panels became available. The luggage rack was also re-designed to hold the roof panels. This example belongs to James Wright

1978–79

In 1978 Corvette danced the
anniversary waltz and in
commemoration of 25 years
production merely re-worked, because
they had nothing new, the existing
model.

A 'fastback' window was added
which greatly improved luggage
capacity, and the interior was given
square, 'flight-deck' styling.

An optional 'Silver Anniversary'
package, as seen on Charles Fausette's
example pictured, consisted of two-
tone silver paint (light over dark),
sport mirrors and aluminium wheels.
'25th Anniversary' emblems with
crossed flags appeared on all models

The Corvette was chosen as the official Indianapolis 500 pace car in 1978 and to commemorate the event, Chevrolet produced a limited edition Pace Car Corvette. This example belonging to Steve Clarke shows that basically it was a cosmetic job with mirrored roof panels, black and silver paint and 'pace car' lettering. Spoilers added suitable drama, while inside, new-style seats were trimmed in silver leather or a combination of silver leather and grey cloth. All Pace Cars came 'fully loaded'

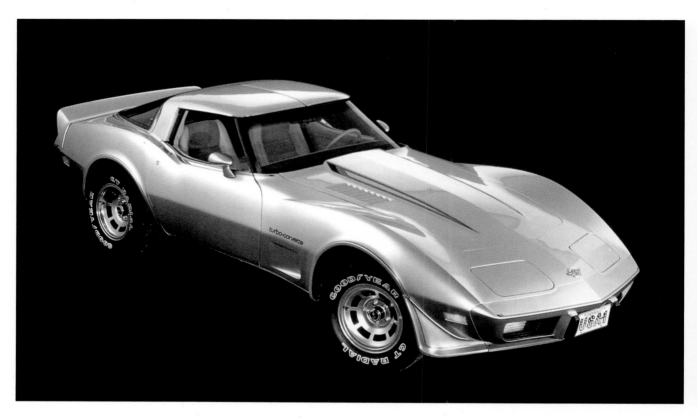

By the end of the seventies, turbocharging appeared to offer 'free' power, and Chevrolet, like most manufacturers, experimented with turbocharging. Their first effort (above), based on a '79 model, featured a single Air Research turbo on a V8. Chevrolet later contracted Specialized Vehicles Inc. to develop turbo versions of the 4.3L V6. Despite several attempts at this with Turbo II and III versions (opposite page), nothing came of the projects and the roll of blowing the Vette fell to Reeves Callaway

1980–82

Below
A significant physcological event in the history of a performance car such as the Corvette was the appearance in 1980 of the infamous '85 mph speedometer'. As if that wasn't a body blow to sports car enthusiasts' egos, then imagine being relegated to a 305 cu. in. V8, as Californians were. It was all in the name of emissions. All other states retained the 350. Outputs for the two engines were 180 and 190 bhp respectively.

Nevertheless, the 1980 models received more attention than other models had, especially in the weight department where engineers trimmed pounds to compensate for the power losses. Nevertheless, air conditioning and tilt/telescopic steering wheels became standard.

Externally, new front and rear bumpers with integral spoilers were added which reduced drag and increased air flow

Left
The turbo Vette re-appeared in 1981 in the form of five specially prepared PPG pace cars for the CART-sanctioned PPG Indy Car World Series. Developed by Chevrolet's Advanced Product Engineering Group, the cars were powered by 229 cu. in. V6s, equipped with Warner-Ishi turbochargers

Above
Californians rejoiced in 1981 because the 350 had finally been certified for sale there. But there were no optional engines available. Tubular stainless steel headers, used the previous year on the 305, were now standard, as was the 'Computer Command Control' system first used in 1980 California Corvettes. Also new for '81 was a reinforced-fibreglass rear leaf spring.

Meanwhile, production ceased in St. Louis and moved, along with many workers, to a new, purpose-built, state-of-the-art plant in Bowling Green, Kentucky. For some months cars were produced in both plants and the total for '81 rose to 45,631 units

Left and above
1982 was far from a mere cosmetic touch-up. For starters, there was 'Crossfire Injection' for the L83 which was good for 10 bhp. At full throttle, solenoid-operated doors in the bonnet directed fresh air directly into the air cleaner.

Also new for '82 was a four-speed automatic transmission with a higher first gear ratio and a torque converter clutch which operated in the three top gears. Manual transmissions were no longer offered.

Probably, because everybody knew a new baby was due, sales tapered off and production, including the 'Collector Edition', fell to 25,407

Previous spread
1982 saw the last of the old and the first of the new because, at last, a sixth generation was being conceived. To honour the coming, Chevrolet offered a built-to-order 'Collector Edition' which enjoyed the benefit of 1963-style wheels, gold and silver treatment inside and out, lifting rear glass, and cloisonne badging. It was the first Corvette to cost more than $20,000 and a mere 6759 were built

1984–85

Below
As far as Chevrolet and the Corvette are concerned, 1983 never happened. 'Long lead' cars were tested by the press in December 1982, and the new generation was introduced in March '83. But, despite its 30th anniversary, there were never any 'official' 1983 Chevrolet Corvettes.

Chevy's game plan was to take on the supercar market, build a Ferrari/Porsche-beater, and in many respects they achieved their aim. For many the '84s were worth the wait. For others though, the new generation was harsh, unreliable, and generally temperamental.

New skin and bones, more muscle, less weight and infinitely longer legs were the order of the day, and they came close. All the car lacked, as it had all its life, was that intangible distinction known as 'class'

Above

The 'Coke-bottle' was all-but indistinguishable in the careful re-design which eliminated all exposed seams as well as the bonnet shutline. Though traditional styling themes were retained, the designers produced a roomier but smaller package with improved visibility and reduced drag (from 0.44 in 1982 to 0.34). The T-top was replaced with a true 'Targa' which stowed in special luggage-bay slots. Also new this year, but not to everybody's taste, were liquid-crystal speed and tacho displays, and digital engine monitoring displays. This example is owned by Erol Halil

Below

Beneath the skin, a new backbone not unlike that pioneered by Lotus. In essence, it retained the traditional layout, but a pressed aluminium C-section spine rigidly connected the independent rear suspension, located now by five rather than three links, to a new Doug Nash '4 + 3 Overdrive' gearbox.

The latter was actually a four-speed transmission with a second set of rear-mounted planetary gears engaged through a hydraulic clutch at the command of the control computer.

There was a console-mounted manual over-ride switch. A no-cost option was the 1982 four-speed, overdrive auto.

Power was provided by the L83 350 now producing 205 bhp.

Supercars are supposed to handle, and it was in this department that Corvette Chief Engineer David R. McLellan and his staff concentrated their efforts. Apart from the above mentioned refinements, they also introduced rack and pinion steering, a single reinforced-fibreglass front leaf spring, and heavy-duty anti-roll bars

front and rear. Tyres were a priority and though designed around the Pirelli P7, the production cars rode on Goodyear Eagle VR50s.

For those who desired the ultimate, there was the Z51 option comprising heavy-duty shocks and lower control arm bushings, uprated front and rear springs and anti-roll bars, and quick-ratio steering. Most drivers, however, found the ride harsh and complained bitterly and loudly. Loud enough to be heard in Bowling Green

Above and left

In an effort to attack the true supercar on its own ground, Chevy built special export versions of the Corvette for Europe, the Middle East, Japan and Latin America. In Europe these models were distinguishable by their 'break-away' sideview mirrors, metric instrumentation, special lights and labels, and a rear panel designed for large license plates. Unfortunately, owners were faced with few franchised dealers, and parts for some of the more temperamental '84s have been almost impossible to come by. Notwithstanding the service problems, there was no doubt in anybody's mind that this was one fast Corvette of which 51,547 examples were produced

Previous spread
*In 1984 Chevrolet announced the
Corvette GTP for the IMSA Camel GT
series. Other than in name, it bore
little resemblance to a road-going
Vette. A mid-mounted, turbocharged
3.8L V6 powered a British, Lola-
developed Kevlar and aluminium
monocoque ground-effect car. Apart
from a pole position at Daytona the
following year, the GTP enjoyed little
success*

Right and below
*Despite the harsh ride and reception,
the new generation evolved rapidly
into a true sports car. For 1985, spring
rates were reduced, even in the Z51
package, and performance was
increased.*

*The 'Crossfire Injection' gave way to
an L98 with mass-airflow sensored,
tuned-port injection producing
230 bhp and 290 lb./ft. of torque.*

*Minor alterations included: re-
positioning the overdrive selection
switch from the dash to the gear lever
knob; revised instrumentation; the
addition of leather sport seats; and
stronger sun-screening for the roof
panel. Production dropped to 39,729*

Far right
*There have been many non-OEM
variations on the Corvette theme over
the years, but none have been more
dramatically different than those built
in Italy by Carrozzeria Bertone.*

*In 1984, to celebrate the
introduction of the sixth generation,
Bertone re-bodied the then-new
Corvette as the Ramarro. Though
decidedly angular when compared to
the traditional Coke-bottle Corvette, it
nevertheless retained the essence of
the new front-end styling*

1986–87

Below
In their continuing effort to legitimize the Corvette as a true world class sports car, Chevrolet engineers continued to refine the product and for the '86 model year introduced anti-lock braking. Also introduced were aluminium cylinder heads which, like those early efforts, were slow to go into production because of problems. They did, however, make it in time for the re-introduction of the convertible, a version of which was used as the 1986 Indy Pace Car

Right
This '86 convertible owned by Paul McNally clearly shows the new centrally-mounted brake light. Less obvious is the 'Vehicle Anti-Theft System' which required a special ignition key which was read electronically. If the wrong key of 15 variants was inserted the car would not start

Right
1986 also saw the re-emergence of the Corvette concept car. Tagged the Corvette Indy, it was, in concept, something of which Duntov would have been proud for the engine, a quad overhead cam, 32-valve V8, was mounted transversely amidships.

Initially designed and prototyped in Detroit under the guidance of chief designer Chuck Jordan, the fibreglass mock-up shown was built in Turin, Italy, in a mere seven weeks. Though not running, the first Indy did hint strongly at the shape and state of the art to come

Far right
The Indy's namesake was this turbocharged, 32-valve, dohc race engine developed by ex-Cosworth engineers Mario Illien and Paul Morgan. The 2.65L Illmor V8 quickly became the Chevrolet Indy V8 and appeared in, amongst others, Roger Penske's team cars.

Though at the time bearing little relation to production engines, the Indy V8 rapidly became a winner, scoring its first victory in the hands of Mario Andretti at the opening race of 1987 at Long Beach, California. It went on to win the championship in both '88 and '89, becoming the most successful powerplant in CART/PPG Indy Car World Series competition. In 1989 alone it boasted 13 pole positions and 13 wins

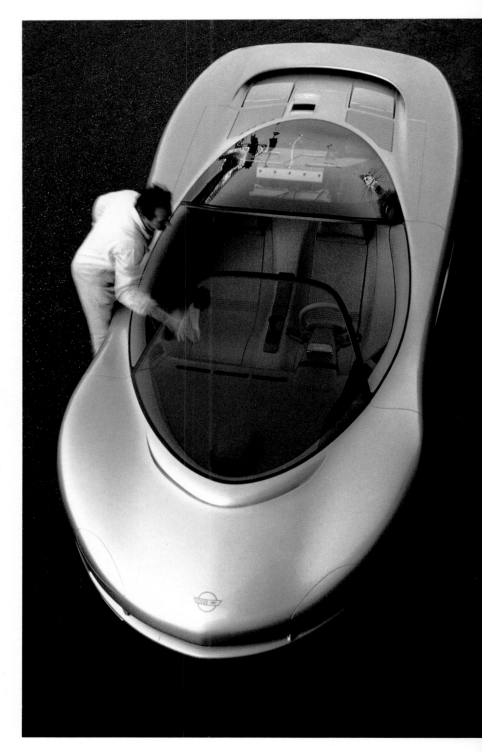

The GTP car was revised for 1986.
However, despite the efforts of
Hendrick Motorsports and hefty
sponsorship from GM's Mr
Goodwrench, the Corvette GTP could
not withstand the might of Nissan's
ZX FTP all-conquering programme

Left
Another year of refinement and confirmation of the Corvette's performance heritage followed in 1987, when the handling packages were once again improved. A new Z52 'sport' kit included Bilstein shocks, 9.5 in. wide wheels, faster steering, larger front anti-roll bar, and convertible-inspired structural changes for coupes. Meanwhile, horsepower increased another 5 points due to the introduction of anti-friction, roller-valve lifters.

On the option list, but rarely fitted because of production problems, was a 'low tyre pressure' indicator.

Though not a factory option, twin-turbo Callaway Corvettes with 345 bhp and claimed top speeds of 178 mph could be specially ordered from Chevrolet dealers

Overleaf
Photographer Mike Key lives but a few miles from the Lotus factory at Hethel in Norfolk, and one day as he was passing the test track he spied this second-generation Corvette Indy undergoing development testing. Neither Lotus nor Chevrolet would comment at the time, but this running concept would be publicly announced the following year

Below
To celebrate 35 years of production, there was a special anniversary edition (coupes only) which featured white paint, white leather seats, white 17 in. wheels, and special commemorative badges

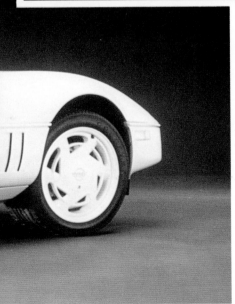

Above
The regular production cars changed
little from the previous year. There
were new dual-piston front brakes,
larger discs and new emergency
brakes which, unlike previous models
where the emergency brake was a
separate drum, now activated the rear
pads. This car is fitted with the 17 in.
wheels which were part of the Z51
handling package

Overleaf
Standard wheels were 16 in. in
diameter, but unlike the roadster, the
coupe could be ordered with a 3.07:1
rear axle ratio which in turn meant
245 bhp. The extra horses came from
a free-flowing exhaust deemed too
loud for roadsters. The Z51 handling
package with larger front brakes,
higher spring rates and a power
steering cooler, could only be ordered
for coupes with manual transmissions.
Production slipped in 1988 to less than
23,000 units

Above
1988 also saw Chevy dealers offer the
IMSA GTO-inspired GTO re-styling
package which fitted all post-1984
Corvettes

Right
In 1987 the Corvette was barred from
the SCCA Showroom Stock Endurance
Series after being undefeated four
years in a row. For a place to race,
Chevy and the SCCA got together for
the Corvette Series—a limited number
of races open to a set number of
identical cars. Chevy specially
equipped 50 and sold them to
individual drivers and teams to
compete for the million dollars in
prize money. Sadly, the Challenge
series came to an end after the 1989
season

Left and above
*Early in 1988, the white, running
prototype photographed in Norfolk
appeared in red in Warren, Michigan.
Heralded as a fully-operational
prototype, this vision of Indy was
powered by a dohc, 32-valve,
sequentially fuel-injected aluminium
V8 code-named 350/32. It was not
dissimilar from the Lotus-developed,
LT5 engine about to debut in the
Corvette ZR-1.*

*Supposedly engineered specifically
for transverse applications, 350/32
featured pent-roof combustion
chambers, chain-driven cams, self-
adjusting hydraulic valves, and a
hydraulic chain tensioner. The*
*induction system employed 16 runners
with 16 Rochester Multec fuel
injectors. GM figures put power output
at 380 bhp.*

*Tractive forces from the engine
were delivered to all four wheels via
three differentials, the central unit
being a viscous coupling providing 35
per cent of the torque to the front
wheels.*

*Active suspension, also developed by
Lotus, employed microprocessor-
controlled hydraulics to eliminate
conventional shocks and springs and
provide the driver with the ability to
optimize handling characteristics.*

Composites featured heavily in the
*construction of the backbone spine,
body platform, and outer skin.*

*Though somewhat underplayed,
Indy was surely tomorrow's technology
today and a glimpse of Corvettes to
come. Or was it?*

ZR-1: the most eagerly-awaited
Corvette of all time, and perhaps, for
Chevrolet, the most frustrating. The
press attacked it like true paparazzi,
heaping praise upon it one minute,
and picking at the warts the next. In
reflection, Chevy should have probably
kept it under wraps until it was ready.
Instead, their excitement led them
almost to slaughter.

On the one hand, the technicalities
of its so-called 'King of the Hill' Lotus-
developed 400 bhp (later rated at
380), 32-valve, four-cam LT5 V8 were
extolled in the media. On the other
hand, its teething troublesome oil
leaks, timing chain problems,
overheating, and failure to meet
emission control regulations
generated as much if not more press.
After a while Chevrolet stopped
calling it 'King of the Hill', and even
as late as March 1990, the company
notified 213 ZR-1 owners that fuel line
leaks could cause engine fires.

The last of the ZR-1's numerous
introductions took place at the 1989
Geneva Motor Show. Meanwhile, a
'sealed' group of cars were introduced
to a select group of journalists in the
South of France where, according to
subsequent reports, all appeared well.
However, the car failed to appear in
showrooms until the end of the year as
a slightly different 1990 model.

Listed at around $55,000, what
examples there were were advertised
for anywhere up to $90,000. Chevrolet
planned to produce around 400 a year,
no doubt making them all immediately
'collectible'. Given time, those first
few 1989 models will probably be
worth as much as those rare '53s

Above
Visually, the ZR-1 is somewhat understated. It is slightly 'blown' at the rear to accommodate the 315/35 ZR-17 Goodyear Eagles and has squared tail-lights in a convex back panel. But essentially the car retains the look of the regular Corvette. Note the absence of a badge on the rear panel. Early cars said LT5, while production cars said ZR-1

A joint effort of GM's C-P-C Group (Chevrolet Motor Division, Group Lotus and Mercury Marine), the LT5 features a unique three-phase, multiple-throttle induction system. Sixteen runners feed air to sequentially-fired fuel injectors targeted over each of the valves.

Within each cylinder, the intake ports, valves and cam lobes are divided into two groups: primary and secondary. Below 3,500 rpm, the engine breathes through the primary ports only. Operation is, in effect, on three valves per cylinder. As the throttle is depressed, so the secondary port throttle valves open to permit the fuel-air mixture to enter the secondary intake valves.

This arrangement produces low-speed tractability and ultimately enough power to push the ZR-1 to speeds in excess of 160 mph

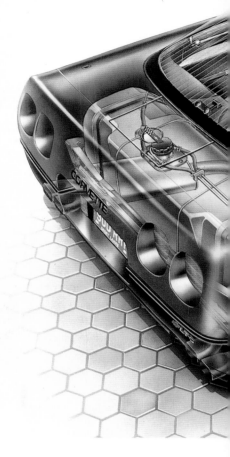

Left
Sacrilege to some but, nevertheless, early in 1989 ZR-1 chassis number 55 was pirated for components to build a LT-5-engined, 1932 Chevy roadster giveaway car for the National Street Rod Association. The roadster was built by renowned dragster chassis builder Woody Gilmore at Chuck Lombardo's California Street Rods. Woody essentially retained the drivetrain components of the ZR-1,

but fabricated his own cantilevered, anti-dive front suspension and housed the whole thing in an all-steel Experi-Metal reproduction '32 Chevy roadster.

Seen here during shakedown runs at Palmdale Raceway, California, the roadster ran mid-13 second quarter miles all day alongside a similarly painted but otherwise stock '89 ZR-1. Photo courtesy of Philippe Danh

Above
This ZR-1, decked-out in police livery, is the Corvette engineer's idea of a joke. It wouldn't be funny if any of the police departments picked it up

Left
Making its debut at the 1990 Geneva Motor Show was Nivola. Nivola was the nickname of Tazio Nuvolari and this exercise by Bertone was painted yellow in honour of the yellow pullover Nuvolari wore while racing in the 1930s and '40s.

In design, Nivola is a long way from the ZR-1. However, it is powered by a mid-mounted LT-5 coupled to a five-speed ZF transaxle. Suspension on all four corners is quadrilateral with electronically-controlled hydro-pneumatic shocks

Above
The 1989 models, such as this convertible owned by Tom Commander, enjoyed the benefits of previous development. For example, the six-speed ZF gearbox used in the ZR-1 became standard, as did the 12-slot, 17 in. wheels. Also new was a 'low tyre pressure' warning system originally announced in 1987.

The Z51 Performance Handling Package, for coupes only, included an FX3 Delco Bilstein Selective Ride Control system which allowed the driver to select one of three ride settings: 'Touring', 'Sport' or 'Performance'. An interim change quickened the steering

Above

Weighing in at 58 lb and a hefty $1,995 was this optional-for-1989 removable hardtop with heated rear window. It was also made available for '86 and newer Corvettes

Above and left

For the new decade, the Corvette's interior received its first major re-design since the 1984 introduction of the sixth generation. The square styling of the previous facia gave way to a new, aircraft-inspired instrument panel which now featured analog as

well as digital gauges. The passenger pad was replaced with air vents, the door trim was changed, and so was the steering wheel. Altogether, it was a more organic interior reflecting contemporary ergonomic trends. There was also a slight increase in horsepower.

At the time of writing a convertible version of the ZR-1 was not an option. However, Don Runkle, vice president of Advanced Engineering, drives an L98 convertible fitted with ZR-1 body panels, the LT5 engine, and a DR-1 insignia on the rear quarter.

True ZR-1 convertibles are being tested and ASC Inc., who will be supplying the convertible componetry, has released pictures of a convertible, but its introduction has been delayed indefinitely

What's in a name? Who cares that the acronym CERV, which originally stood for Chevrolet Experimental Racing Vehicle, now stands for Corporate Experimental Research Vehicle. CERV III is the latest chapter in the ongoing Corvette Indy story.

Engineered at Lotus, CERV III is powered by a transverse, mid-mounted, twin-turbo, intercooled 650 bhp version of the LT5. The transmission is basically a three-speed Turbo-Hydramatic mated to a two-speed gearbox giving six speeds in total. A central viscous coupling splits the drive between front and rear, while torque split is determined by a computer-controlled hydrostatic device.

The central backbone is a carbon-fibre torque tube weighing only 38 lb. Its ends are machined from titanium and support full, computer-controlled active suspension. Stopping power is by carbon-on-carbon brakes which feature twin carbon discs gripped by internal calipers with carbon pads

Above

Looking very 'hand-built', the facia of CERV III has a full array of high-visibility analog instruments. In addition, a sophisticated navigation system and a message centre capable of displaying not only warning advisories but also a wide variety of operational information: engine diagnostics, active suspension parameters, torque split, individual wheel steer angles, and various performance measurements

Below
CERV III—with its mid-mounted, transverse, twin-turbo 650 bhp version of the LT5, lightweight construction, active suspension and interactive control—could be a precursor for Corvettes to come

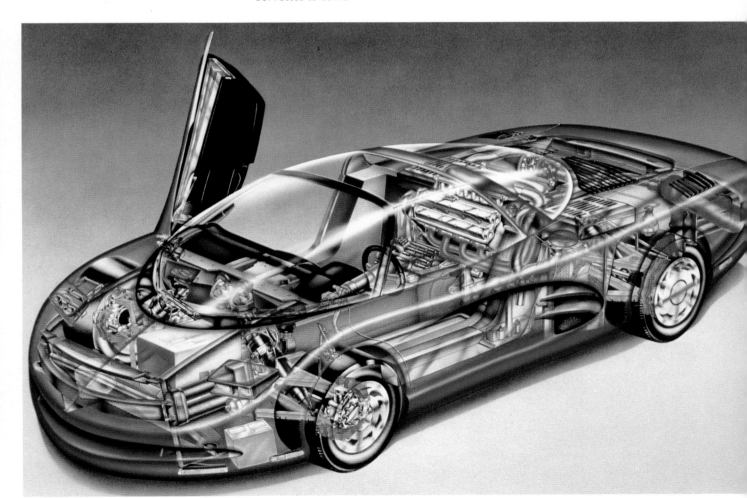

Above

In March 1990, to prove a point, Tommy Morrison took two Corvettes, an L98 and a ZR-1, to a test facility in Fort Stockton, Texas for an assault on several world records. With a team of eight drivers, the almost stock ZR-1 (the blueprinted engine failed to arrive in time) ran for 24 hours at an average speed of 175.885 mph. It ran on for another four hours, 12 minutes to cover a total of 5,000 trouble-free miles

Right

Chevrolet surprised everybody at the 1991 long-lead press preview, held at Michigan International Speedway in June 1990, for they displayed a very much re-styled Corvette. A new, smooth front end featured wrap-around lights, the gills were four in number and horizontal instead of two and vertical, and the rub strip was wider and painted body colour. At the rear, all Corvettes now had the squared-off ZR-1-style tail-lights and a de-bossed Corvette logo. L98 cars, however, remained narrower in the rear than their ZR-1 counterparts. New, one-piece directional wheels, first seen on the CERV III concept car, became standard on all models. There was no power increase

And beyond . . .

What's in the Chevrolet store of the future? Well, despite all the mid-engine ballyhoo, Zora Arkus-Duntov is unlikely to see his dream come true. Chevrolet has certainly spent a lot of money on the Indy/CERV III programmes, but all indications are that the foreseeable generations will retain the present front engine/rear drive configuration. Certainly much of the chassis technology gleaned from those concepts will find its way, as it is already doing, into production. But a mid-engined Corvette, unless it's a limited-edition Porsche 959/Ferrari F40 exercise, appears unlikely. However, at the 1990 long-lead press preview, when asked about a possible mid-engined Corvette, engineers said, 'It's not out of the question.'

New models proposed for 1991 introduction have been pushed back because of ZR-1 problems to at least 1993, probably 1995. A complete re-design for mid-to-late decade introduction is underway. Photographs of two different full-size clay models have been seen (see below) and indications are that they retain front-engined V8 power.

Nobody is saying exactly which engines will be offered. Rumours abound regarding everything from more powerful Gen II small blocks, recognizable by their front-mounted distributor and low-level throttle-body injection, which are expected in '92, to developments of the LT5 which will appear with 400 bhp as originally specified. A big-block Corvette, nicknamed 'Big Doggie', has been spotted at the Arizona proving grounds, and there is talk of Cadillac's North Star 32-valve V8 finding its way into the Corvette. Meanwhile, Dow Chemical has announced a lightweight magnesium small-block V8 which is undergoing evaluation in a Vette.

At this stage, only those engineers directly involved with the Corvette have any idea about what to expect. One thing is for sure though, the next generation will provide yet another interesting chapter in Corvette evolution.

Below
The 1995 Chevrolet Corvette? Time will tell . . .